Children in our World

REFUGEES AND MIGRANTS

Ceri Roberts

Hanane Kai

B.E.S.

PUBLISHING

First edition for the United States and Canada published in 2017
by Barron's Educational Series, Inc.

First published in Great Britain in 2016 by Wayland

Wayland is an imprint of Hachette Children's Books,
part of Hodder & Stoughton.
A Hachette U.K. company.
www.hachette.co.uk
www.hachettechildrens.co.uk

Text © Wayland, 2016
Written by Ceri Roberts
Illustrations © Hanane Kai, 2016

Texturing of illustrations by Sarah Habli
Additional illustration work by Ashley Choukeir
Edited by Corinne Lucas
Designed by Sophie Wilkins

All inquiries should be addressed to:
Peterson's Publishing, LLC
8740 Lucent Boulevard, Suite 400
Highlands Ranch, CO 80129
www.petersonsbooks.com

ISBN: 978-1-4380-5020-1

Library of Congress Control No.: 2017935870

Date of Manufacture: January 2020
Manufactured by: WKT Co. Ltd., Shenzhen, China

Printed in China
9 8 7 6 5 4 3

Contents

Who are refugees and migrants?

Your home is the place where you spend time with the people you love, eat your favorite food, play with toys, and sleep in a warm bed.

Sometimes people leave their homes because wars, natural disasters, or acts of terrorism have made it too dangerous to stay. These people are known as refugees. Others leave for a happier, healthier life, to join family members overseas, or because they don't have enough money and need a job. People who choose to do this are called migrants.

Not all migrants leave home because they are living in poverty, but this book will look at the different reasons why people need to escape to other countries and what happens to them afterward.

Children on the move

Some refugees and migrants are children who travel with parents or guardians, but every year tens of thousands of children make long journeys without grown-ups. This is usually because they are orphans, or because they were separated from their parents along the way.

If you've ever lost your mom or dad for a few minutes at the park or store, you know how scary it feels when you're by yourself. It's much harder for children who are alone in a strange country. They often don't speak the language or have anywhere to sleep, and they miss their family and friends.

Where do they come from?

Refugees and migrants travel from countries all over the world.
Some flee because of terrorism and war. Others leave because
their lives are at risk because of who they are or what they believe.

Often, refugees and migrants come from developing countries where
people don't live long lives or have much money, and where many
children don't go to school. Sometimes their homes have been
destroyed by natural disasters, such as hurricanes, earthquakes,
or floods.

Leaving home behind

If you've ever moved, you know it's normal to pack up your belongings and take them with you. When you go on vacation, you fill a suitcase with your clothes and toys. Refugees usually leave their homes in a hurry, so they don't have time to pack. Even if they do, they can't carry heavy bags over long distances. Some manage to take a small bag with them, but this can get lost along the way. Most have nothing left to remind them of home.

Many refugees and migrants don't have a passport or a visa, which are the documents you need to enter another country. This means they aren't allowed to travel by plane, so their journey can take weeks, or even months.

12

How do they travel?

Refugees and migrants are often so desperate that they risk their lives and pay smugglers to transport them to another country. Some spend days hidden in a truck without food or water. They have to keep very quiet and are scared that they might be found.

Others travel across rough seas in overcrowded boats. Many more walk for weeks in extreme weather conditions, without warm clothes, rain gear, or anywhere to sleep. Sadly, some don't survive the dangerous journey. It's important that we find ways to help so that they won't have to put themselves in danger.

Where are they going?

Refugees and migrants want to live in a country where they feel safe.

Just like everyone else, they dream of a warm, comfortable home, to take care of their family, to get a job, or to go to school. Only then will they be able to do the everyday things that we take for granted, such as buying their favorite foods, watching television, and having fun with friends.

What happens when they arrive?

Most refugees and migrants have only the clothes they are wearing. Usually, they have no money or anywhere to stay. It's hard to get help when they don't know who to ask or how to speak the country's language.

This is why many refugees and migrants end up homeless or living in tents, trailers, or shacks in refugee camps. Although this isn't as comfortable as living in a house, there are lots of helpers who hand out food, clothing, and medicine to people.

Life in refugee camps

If you've been camping, you probably had lots of fun, but life in refugee camps is very hard. Families have to live together in small spaces, and children don't have their own room, or even their own bed. Some don't have a bed at all.

In some places, it's very hot in the summer and very cold in the winter. There's no electricity or running water, so it's difficult to keep clean. People have to wait in line for hours for food or medicine, and there are no schools.

Refugee camps are home to thousands of people, and some families live there for many years. This is why doctors, nurses, teachers, and other volunteers go to help people settle in, build communities and schools, and stay healthy.

People who help

Teams of volunteers from charities and government organizations work hard to help people who are living in refugee camps. Some doctors and nurses set up clinics where they can treat people who are sick. Other volunteers help build shelters, or they set up schools for children. Many more people help by collecting clothes or food.

Seeking asylum

When a refugee or migrant arrives in a new country, they have to ask the government for permission to stay. This is called "seeking asylum." It can be very complicated and confusing.

Governments help asylum seekers find places to live and give them a small amount of money for food and other things they need. Asylum seekers who are children, traveling without an adult, usually live in children's homes or with foster families, who keep them safe.

Not all asylum seekers are allowed to stay in a country, so they might ask the government for permission again, seek asylum in another country, or live in refugee camps. Some are sent back to their home country.

A new life

When asylum is given, people gain official refugee status. This means that they can stay in their new country for a number of years. During this time, they can work to earn money and create a better life for their family. Children can go to school, where they make new friends and sometimes learn a new language. So, if you meet a new child at school from another country, it's important to make them feel welcome.

If, after a period of time, it's still not safe for refugees to return to their home country, they can apply to stay forever. This means that they won't have to worry about the future, and they can enjoy a safe and happy life in their new home.

Talk about your worries

It's good to care about other people, but it can be upsetting to think about what life is like for refugees and migrants. If you are sad or worried, it is important to talk to an adult about how you feel. Together, you can think about ways that you can help.

Remember, most people have a safe and comfortable home to live in. You and your family are not at great risk of becoming refugees or migrants. There are lots of smart people working hard to stop wars and terrorism, and to end poverty all around the world. They want to make sure that everyone can live happily.

How you can help

Lots of people are already helping refugees and migrants, but there are many ways that you could help, too. You could collect food, clothes, toys, or books to send to refugee camps. You could organize a bake sale or take part in a sponsored challenge to raise money for charities that help refugees. You could even write a letter to the government asking them to do more to look after people in need.

Find out more

Books

Teacup
Rebecca Young, Dial Books, 2016

Lost and Found Cat: The True Story of Kunkush's Incredible Journey
Doug Kuntz and Amy Shrodes, Crown Books for Young Readers, 2017

Inside Out and Back Again
Thanhha Lai, HarperCollins, 2011

Websites

Care International helps refugees around the world.
www.careinternational.org

The International Rescue Committee helps people who are affected by conflict and disaster.
www.rescue.org

Unicef helps protect children who are in danger.
www.unicef.org

Save the Children works to protect children in need all over the world.
www.savethechildren.org

The Red Cross is a charity that helps victims of war and disaster.
www.redcross.org

The American Refugee Committee creates programs and offers services for refugees and refugee communities across the globe.
www.arcrelief.org

The Canadian Council for Refugees is committed to the rights and protection of refugees and migrants in Canada and around the world.
www.ccrweb.ca

Glossary

asylum protection given by a country to a person who has left his or her home country as a refugee

charity a group that helps people in need

developing countries places in the world where people rely mostly on farming for food, earn very little money, do not always go to school, and have little or no health care

foster family people who take care of children when their parents can't

government a group of people who control and make decisions for a country

migrant a person who leaves his or her home country to find a better life

natural disasters natural events that cause great damage, such as hurricanes, floods, and earthquakes

orphan a child whose mother and father have died

refugee a person who leaves his or her home country to find a safer place to live

refugee camp a place where refugees can stay when they have escaped their home country

smugglers people who secretly take things, or other people, to a different place

terrorism the use of violent acts to scare people and to make them do things they don't want to do

volunteer someone who gives up their time to help other people without being paid

war when states or nations fight against each other

Index